Distant Lands

TELLING tales
in Latin Part 2

by Lorna Robinson

Illustrated by Soham De

This book is dedicated to all the students who haunt the classics centre at Cheney School - LR

Contents

Acknowledgements

I would like thank David Hodgkinson and Nathan Pinkoski for kindly reading a final draft of this book. I would also like to thank Evelien Bracke and David Gimson for reading through multiple proofs, and for providing friendship, support and encouragement for this and other classical endeavours.

Finally, I would like to thank my parents, my husband Duncan and my daughter Rachel, for their love, and for putting up with all the time I spent on this and all the hot chocolate I drank while doing it. - LR

I would like to thank my parents for their support and love. To Prachi for her assistance, contribution and keeping me company during late hours at work. - SD

In my last little set of tales, you might remember that I mentioned that I ended up going to faraway lands. It's a rather sad story, which is why, when I wrote about it, I called the poems "Tristia", which means "the sad things".

The Roman emperor of my time, Augustus, a clever and powerful man, decided to send me to a place at the edges of his mighty empire, called Tomi. It was a "carmen" and "error" that led to my unhappy exile, and that is all I can say about the whole matter.

If you'd like to know more, and also to hear more magical tales, then join me as we go together to faraway places.

Tempestas

This story begins on the way to Tomi, a dark, rainy, gloomy corner of the Roman Empire. Banished from the light and warmth of my beloved Roma, I found myself on a ship, crossing the steely grey ocean, heading to a place I had never been, where I would probably spend the rest of my life.

And to make matters worse, a storm arose along the journey...

Dei oceani et caeli—quid enim nisi vota supersunt?—
nolite solvere membra quassatae navis.
me miserum, quanti montes aquarum volvunt!
iam undae paene stellas summas tangunt.
quantae valles subsidunt!
iam paene Tartarum nigrum tangunt.
quocumque aspicio, nihil est, nisi oceanus et aer.
inter utrum, magni venti fremunt.
dum dico, unda meum vultum obruit.

New grammar

Before you start translating, I need to let you know about some new noun endings. In my last set of tales, you met the subject, object and also dative endings for nouns. In this passage, you can find examples of a new ending, called the genitive ending. Here is an example:

montes **aquarum** = mountains of **waters**

The **genitive** ending, among other things, shows possession, and is translated as "of…". Here are the endings you have learned so far:

Group 1	Group 2	Group 2(n)	Group 3
stella	amicus	templum	navis (nominative/subject)
stellam	amicum	templum	navem (accusative/object)
stellae	amici	templi	navis (genitive)
stellae	amico	templo	navi (dative)
stellae	amici	templa	naves (nom. pl.)
stellas	amicos	templa	naves (acc. pl.)
stellarum	amicorum	templorum	navium (gen. pl.)
stellis	amicis	templis	navibus (dat. pl.)

As you can see, some endings are the same so you need to think hard about what makes sense in the context of the sentence – it's like piecing together a puzzle! Can you pick out which endings look the same?

Here is a sentence from the passage:

nolite solvere membra **quassatae navis**!

Don't loosen the limbs **of the shaken ship**!

The word 'navis' is genitive here, but it could have been nominative (i.e. the subject). The command "don't loosen" tells us that we don't need a subject, though, and we have an object, 'limbs' ('membra'). This process of thinking through how the sentence could work will show you which case the noun is in. Another clue to this is the adjective 'quassatae'('shaken'). This looks like a group 1 ending, which means it is agreeing with a feminine noun. It could therefore be describing a subject in the plural, but there isn't any noun like this in the sentence.

It could be a dative singular ending but there is nothing in the sentence which points at that. So it must be a genitive singular ending – which fits perfectly with 'navis' if 'navis' is genitive. The jigsaw is falling into place!

Right, now have a look at the rest of the words!

Vocabulary

me miserum = wretched me!
niger, nigra, nigrum = black
nisi = except
nolite solvere = "don't loosen!"
obruo (3) = I rush against
paene = almost
quantus/a/um = how great
quassatus/a/um = shaken
quid = what?
quocumque = wherever
membrum (2) = limb
navis, navis (3) = ship
stella (1) = star
subsido (3) = I settle, subside
summus/a/um = highest
utrum = each
vallis, vallis (3) = valley
volvo (3) = I roll
votum (2) = prayer

You will notice from now on that whenever I list a noun from group 3, I will list the genitive of the word as well. This is because the word often changes a bit, so it makes it easier to recognise other forms of the same word.

So here I was, heading away from my beloved Roma, on a ship that was creaking and rocking in the storm. Salt water was being hurled into my face, and I was wondering if I would ever see land again. It was pretty miserable. What made it harder to bear was my destination…

non ego avidus pecuniam quaero,
nec Athenas peto, ubi, ut puer, studui.
non urbes Asiae, non loca visa prius, quaero;
nec urbem Alexandriae peto, nec videre Nilum.
necesse est mihi ire ad litora Nigri Ponti.
necesse est mihi videre Tomitas! ubi in orbe locus est? nescio.

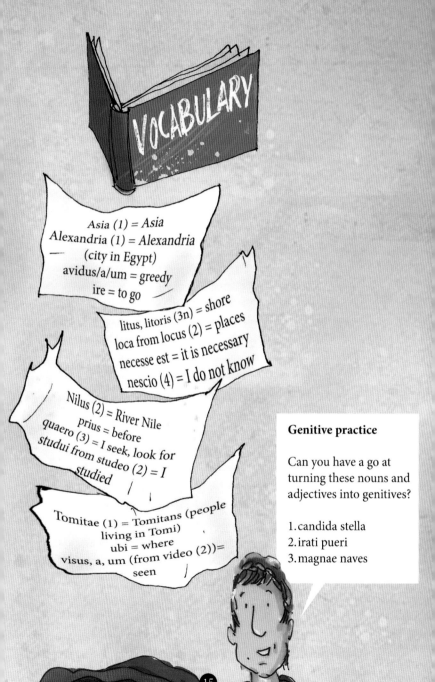

VOCABULARY

Asia (1) = Asia
Alexandria (1) = Alexandria
— (city in Egypt)
avidus/a/um = greedy
ire = to go

litus, litoris (3n) = shore
loca from locus (2) = places
necesse est = it is necessary
nescio (4) = I do not know

Nilus (2) = River Nile
prius = before
quaero (3) = I seek, look for
studui from studeo (2) = I
studied

Tomitae (1) = Tomitans (people
living in Tomi)
ubi = where
visus, a, um (from video (2)) =
seen

Genitive practice

Can you have a go at
turning these nouns and
adjectives into genitives?

1. candida stella
2. irati pueri
3. magnae naves

15

Activities

When I was travelling to Tomi, it felt such a long way from Roma – like the other end of the world! Can you find a map and locate Rome and Tomi on it – perhaps you could draw your own floor map and plot my stormy course across the ocean. You could make a Roman boat and play a game to move it along, with 'storm' cards!

I mention other places I had travelled to in this chapter – can you also find them on a map – and maybe you could make them part of your game too?

Maybe, like me, you have spent time away from your home, and visited a place you found strange – you could use your experience and imagination to write a log of each day of my journey – how would you have felt if you were me? What would have been your fears?

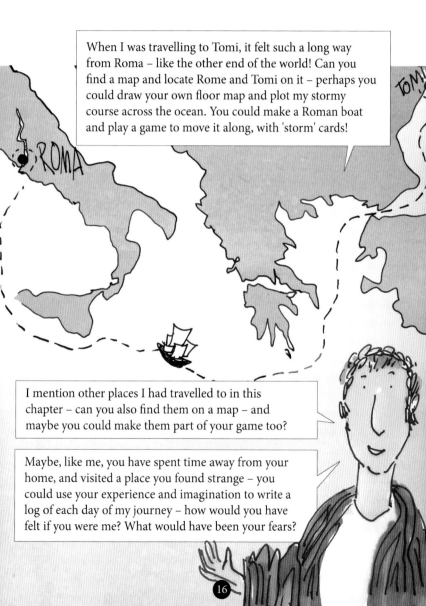

I had never seen or heard of Tomi before I was sent there, so I had lots of wild imaginings about what it might look like, and what the people who lived there might have been like. Why don't you draw a picture or write a description of how you imagine it to be? Later in the book, you'll get a chance to see how close you were!

chapter duo
Lycaon

One of the things I spent a lot of time doing on my journey to Tomi, as well as during my time there, was to think of the stories I had told. Sometimes I would use them to make new stories or to explain ideas, just to amuse myself.

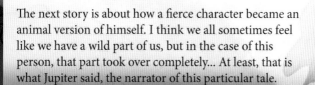

The next story is about how a fierce character became an animal version of himself. I think we all sometimes feel like we have a wild part of us, but in the case of this person, that part took over completely... At least, that is what Jupiter said, the narrator of this particular tale.

"ego deus sub humana imagine terras visitabam.
longa mora est enumerare scelera virorum.
nocte intravi, et signa dei dedi. sed vir Lycaon risit et dixit:
"nunc utrum deum an virum probo."
Lycaon iugulum viri gladio scidit! partim corpus aquis
mollit, partim igni torruit.
simul in mensa posuit, ego vindice flamma domum delevi."

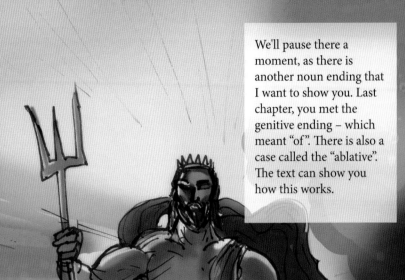

We'll pause there a moment, as there is another noun ending that I want to show you. Last chapter, you met the genitive ending – which meant "of". There is also a case called the "ablative". The text can show you how this works.

Jupiter describes how he came down to earth in disguise – "**sub humana imagine**", which literally means "**under human form**".

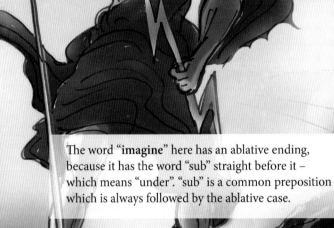

The word "**imagine**" here has an ablative ending, because it has the word "sub" straight before it – which means "under". "sub" is a common preposition which is always followed by the ablative case.

Here's another example from the story: "**gladio**". Here, this means "**with a sword**" and is in the ablative case. The ablative case expresses things like where a noun is located, or how it is being used, e.g. "in", "by", "with" etc. Here are the endings, which, as you can see, are often the same as other case endings. You need to think about the context to work it out. There are some sentences to practise this below.

New grammar

Group 1	Group 2	Group 3
stella	amicus	navis (nominative/subject)
stellam	amicum	navem (accusative/object)
stellae	amici	navis (genitive)
stellae	amico	navi (dative)
stella	amico	nave (ablative)
stellae	amici	naves (nom. pl.)
stellas	amicos	naves (acc. pl.)
stellarum	amicorum	navium (gen. pl.)
stellis	amicis	navibus (dat. pl.)
stellis	amicis	navibus (abl. pl.)

Vocabulary

atque = and

deleo (2) = I destroy

enumero (1) = I count

flamma (1) = flame

imago, imaginis (3) = form, image

iugulum (2n) = throat

mensa (1) = table

mora (1) = delay

partim... partim... = some of... some of...

probo (1) = I prove

scelus, sceleris (3n) = crime

scindo (3) = I cut

torreo (2) = I bake, roast

simul = as soon as

utrum... an... = whether.... or...

vindex, vindicis = vengeful

Jupiter continues his gruesome story, with the villainous Lycaon fleeing into the night.

"territus Lycaon in silentium ruris fugit.
Lycaon dicere non potest, et frustra exululat.
in pecudes currit et nunc quoque sanguine gaudet.
vestes in villos, lacerti in crura vertunt:
Lycaon fit lupus, sed vestigia veteris formae servat.
canitiem eandem habet, eundem violentum vultum habet.
idem oculi lucent, eadem imago feritatis est."

Here are some sentences to practice spotting and translating the ablative case!
1. femina magna voce dixit.
2. lupus in agris currebat.
3. sunt multae stellae in caelo.

Can you turn these nouns and adjectives into ablatives?
1. laeti lupi
2. solus vir
3. candida stella

Vocabulary

canities (5) = white hair
crus, cruris (3n) = a leg
eandem/eundem/idem = the same
exululo (1) = I howl
feritas, feritatis (3) = ferocity, wildness
fio = I become
frustra = in vain
gaudeo (2) = I rejoice
habeo (2) = I have
luceo (2) = I gleam
lupus (2) = wolf
pecus, pecudis (3) = flock
rus, ruris (3n) = countryside
sanguis, sanguinis (3) = blood
sed = but
servo (1) = I keep
silentium (2) = silence
vestis, vestis (3) = clothes
vestigia (2) = traces
vetus, veteris = old
violentus/a/um = violent
villus (2) = hair

Activities

It sounds a lot like Lycaon got what he deserved, doesn't it? He was a savage murderer, and then he was magically transformed into a wolf, who delighted in killing and bloodshed.

Jupiter is the narrator of this particular tale, though, and he is using it as an example to the other gods of why humankind are wicked and should be punished. Do you think this affects how he tells the tale? Does he omit some bits and emphasise others to suit his purpose? Do you ever do that when retelling an event?

You could have a go at telling this story from the perspective of Lycaon himself. How might the story be different from Lycaon's perspective, and what different bits of the tale do you think you might emphasise or even add to tell a different account?

This story is an example of someone turning into something that expresses their inner character in animal form. Can you think of any other stories of transformation that also do this? Perhaps you could make up your own? Who might turn into what, and why?

The story of Lycaon, like many of my tales, can be turned into a play or event enacted as a dance – maybe you could have a go at writing a play or developing a series of dance moves to express the gradual or rapid change from man to wolf!

See you in the next story...

chapter tres
Suprema nox in Roma

Back to my stormy seas and creaking ship again. When I didn't
manage to distract myself with magical tales, I often found myself
reminiscing about Roma, and wishing I was there. One thing I often
did was relive my last evening there. It was the last time I saw my wife
and loyal friends, and the last moments I spent in that beautiful city I
call home. Here is what I remember of that night…

Cum tristis imago illius noctis subit,
quae mihi supremum tempus in urbe fuit,
cum repeto noctem, qua tot caras res reliqui,
ex meis oculis nunc quoque gutta cadit.
iam prope lux aderat, qua Caesar me discedere
finibus extremae Ausoniae iussit.

Vocabulary

aderat = from adsum = was present
cado (3) = I fall
carus/a/um = dear
discedo (3) = I go away
extremus/a/um = far, extreme
finis, finis (3) = end
gutta (1) = tear
illius – genitive from ille = of that
iussit from iubeo = he ordered
nunc = now
qua = in which
quae = which
repeto (3) = I recall
subit from subeo = emerged
supremus/a/um = final
tempus, temporis (3n) = time
tot = so many
tristis/e = sad

Do you remember that these poems which I wrote about being sent away are called 'tristia' meaning "sad things"?

This word comes from the adjective 'tristis' meaning 'sad'. You have met lots of adjectives before – such as 'laetus, a, um' meaning 'happy', and 'magnus, a, um' meaning 'big'. These are all adjectives which behave like either group one nouns (if agreeing with a feminine noun), or group two nouns if agreeing with a masculine or neuter noun). For example, these phrases:

magna gutta
parvus puer
laetae feminae

Can you translate these?

There are also adjectives which behave like group three nouns, such as 'tristis' meaning 'sad' and 'ferox' meaning 'fierce'. There are lots of small variations between these adjectives – some have different endings for masculine, feminine and neuter, whereas others, like 'tristis', have a same endings for masculine and feminine.

For now, I'm going to show you how words like 'tristis' work:

	MASC/FEM	NEUTER
Nom.	tristis	triste
Acc.	tristem	triste
Gen.	tristis	tristis
Dat.	tristi	tristi
Abl.	tristi	tristi
Nom. plural	tristes	tristia
Acc. plural	tristes	tristia
Gen. plural	tristium	tristium
Dat. plural	tristibus	tristibus
Abl. plural	tristibus	tristibus

stupui - qualis me Iuppiter ignibus percutit.
vivebam - sed eram nescius meae vitae.
ubi tamen dolor ipse nubem removit,
et tandem sensus mei convaluerunt,
tristibus amicis dixi, qui iam erant pauci.
mea uxor lacrimabat et me tenebat,
sed filia procul in oris Libycis aberat.
de meo exilio non sciebat. ubique lacrimae sonabant.

Vocabulary

convaleo (2) = I recover
eram = I was
exilium (2) = exile
in oris Libycis = on Libyan shores
lacrima (1) = tear
lacrimo (1) = I cry
nubes, nubis (3) = cloud
percutio (4) = I strike
procul = far away
sono (1) = I resound
sensus (4) = senses
ubique = on all sides
vivo (3) = I live
vita (1) = life

Activities

It's still difficult for me to think about that evening, since it was the last time I saw my family and friends. It was also hard to say goodbye to my life and my world and all my things. I had to think very carefully about what I would take with me, and what I would leave behind. Imagine you were going away for a long time – what ten things would you choose to take with you, and why would you take those particular things? Try making a list – you'll soon see how difficult it is to do!

At the start of the second part of the story, I explained how I felt as if I had been struck by a thunderbolt from Jupiter himself, and as a result, I was dazed and didn't know what to do or where I was for a while. Have you ever felt like that?

Perhaps you could imagine having received a surprise that would change your life – it could be good or bad. How would you feel in the first hours after hearing? What emotions would you feel? Write an account of it.

I spoke of a thunderbolt as this was Jupiter's weapon – this is because Jupiter is a sky god

What are the weapons or associated objects of the other Olympian gods and goddesses?

And what are their domains – sky? Sea?

33

Can you think of a fun way of displaying all this information? You could create a set of cards for the various gods and goddesses, perhaps.

I am comparing the message of the exile with being struck by a thunderbolt – this is called a simile.

34

Can you think of any other similes that might work for describing surprise – whether bad and good.

An example might be comparing surprise to suddenly falling into cold water, or perhaps something like a loud bang that hurts your ears and causes everything to sound muffled for a while so you're walking around in a slightly dreamlike state?

chapter quattuor
Pyramus et Thisbe

Being so far from my wife, my mind was often drawn to the tales of impossible or forbidden love that I had told in my poems. One of my favourite of these stories is that of Pyramus and Thisbe. These two lovers from Babylon were forbidden to be together by their parents, but found a clever way of communicating...

Pyramus et Thisbe, alter pulcherrimus iuvenis,
altera pulcherrima puella, in Oriente habitabant.
contiguas villas tenebant. vicinia notitiam fecit,
tempore amor crevit. sed patres amorem vetuerunt.
murus inter villas tenuem rimam habebat.
nemo per saecula longa rimam notavit -
sed quid amor non sentit? primi amantes rimam viderunt.
per rimam blanditiae transire murmure minimo solebant.

Vocabulary

alter... altera... = one... the other...
amantes = the lovers
blanditiae (1) = sweet words
contiguus, a, um = neighbouring
crevit **from cresco** = grew
fecit **from facio** = made
habito (1) = I live
iuvenis, iuvenis (3) = young man
minimus/a/um = smallest, very small
murus (2) = wall
notitia (1) = acquaintance, notice
in Oriente = in the East
pulcherrimus/a/um = most beautiful, very
beautiful
rima (1) = crack
saeculum (2) = age, time
tenuis/e = thin
vetuerunt **from veto** = forbade
vicinia (1) = proximity, closeness

Comparatives and Superlatives

In the first sentence, you will have noticed the same adjective describing both Pyramus and Thisbe. You may remember from my first set of stories an adjective "pulcher" meaning "beautiful". "pulcherrimus" is called the **superlative** which means that you say "the most" or "very" before the adjective. You can also use a **comparative** form of an adjective where you say "more" in front of the adjective. Here are some examples, so you can see what I mean:

ADJECTIVE	COMPARATIVE	SUPERLATIVE
laetus, a, um (happy)	laetior (happier, more happy)	laetissimus, a, um (happiest, very ha
tristis, is, e (sad)	tristior (more sad, sadder)	tristissimus, a, um (saddest, very sac
pulcher, ra, rum	pulchrior	pulcherrimus, a, um
sollicitus, a, um	sollicitior	sollicitissimus, a, um

And, of course, there are the wild ones, which never behave as you would expect. One is in this passage, and you'll come upon many more on your travels. Here are a few:

ADJECTIVE	COMPARATIVE	SUPERLATIVE
magnus, a, um (big)	maior (bigger)	maximus, a, um (biggest, very big)
parvus, a, um (small)	minor (smaller)	minimus, a, um (smallest, very smal

Do you think you'll be able to recognise these forms now? See if you can spot any in the next part of the story, as our doomed lovers hatch a plan.

Pyramus et Thisbe excedere nocte coniuraverunt:
convenire ad tumulum Nini constituerunt.
arbor ibi erat uberrima pomis niveis. latere sub umbra
arboris constituerunt.
callidissima Thisbe, vultu adoperto, ad tumulum
pervenit. Thisbe sub arbore sedit.
ecce! leo venit. procul Thisbe leonem vidit et in
antrum fugit. dum fugit, velamen reliquit.

Did you spot any superlatives in the passage? There were a couple hanging around to see. Here is some more vocabulary to help you:

Vocabulary

adopertus/a/um = covered
antrum (2) = cave
callidus, a, um = crafty
coniuro (1) = I plot, plan
constituo (3) = I decide
dum = while
fugo (1) = I flee
latere **from lateo** = to hide
leo, leonis (3) = lion
Ninus = Ninus, founder of the ancient city of Nineveh
niveus/a/m = snow white
pervenio (4) = I reach
pomum (2) = fruit (apples, berries, nuts, figs, dates etc.)
procul = from a distance
reliquit **from relinquo** = she left
tumulus (2) = tomb
uber = rich, fruitful
velamen, velaminis (3n) = veil

Poor Thisbe must have been very frightened. I wonder if you can guess what is going to happen? Let's carry on with the tale.

Pyramus ad tumulum serius pervenit. vestigia leonis vidit et palluit. tum vero velamen invenit. "una nox duos amantes delet!" iuvenis clamavit. Pyramus velamen ad umbram arboris portavit. oscula velamini dedit, et tum in sua ilia gladium demisit.

amantes = lovers
clamo (1) = I shout
demitto (3) = I thrust
ilia (2) = insides
palluit **from palleo** = he grew pale
porto (1) = I carry
serius = later
vero = indeed

So Pyramus had taken his life in despair because he believed Thisbe to have been killed by the lion; and they say that the snow-white berries of the mulberry tree turned crimson from the blood of Pyramus. Thisbe in turn then found Pyramus, and took her own life, so one night really did destroy the two young lovers, and from then on mulberries turn red when they ripen. Such is the legacy of the sorry tale!

Activities

This particular story is set in the ancient city of Babylon. Can you find out where Babylon is?

You might also remember that the two lovers are due to meet at the tomb of Ninus – can you find out who he is?

There are other very well-known stories of lovers, forbidden to see each other by their families, who create a secret plan, and in the course of carrying it out, mistakenly think that the other has died and then take their own lives. Can you think of other stories like this? Make a list of the key aspects of the plot. These stories are often called 'tragedies' – where does the word 'tragedy' come from?

Can you write your own tragic story – where would it be set, and how would the plot unfold?

This story combines a tragedy with a story that explains something about the world – we met some of these in my last set of tales – can you remember what this type of story is called?

In this case, it explains how mulberries start off white and then when ripe, they become reddish. Can you create a story around the ripening of a fruit or some other plant?

See you back on my ship…

chapter quinque

Hiems

After what seemed like an endless and uncertain voyage, finally we sighted land on the grey and rainy horizon. It was a land I had never seen before and I had no idea what I would find when we finally reached the sandy beach. It was not long before I began to experience what the long, cold, bleak winters were like, so different from the ones I knew in my longed-for, distant **Roma**.

quis adhuc Nasonis adempti meminit?
meumne nomen sine me in urbe superest?
ego in hac barbaria habito. hic stellae numquam oceanum tangunt.
dum tamen aura tepet, Hister nostros defendit. ille bella suis aquis repellit.
sed tum tristis hiems acerbum caput tollit.
terra est candida marmoreo gelu!
tremens caelum has gentes premit.

Here's some icy, gloomy
vocabulary for you:

Vocabulary

acerbus, a, um = bitter, gloomy
ademptus, a, um = banished
caelum (2) = sky
barbaria (1) = barbarity
bellum (2) = war
defendo (3) = I defend
gelu, gelus (3n) = ice
gens, gentis (3) = tribe
hac = this
has = these
hic = here
hiems, hiemis (3) = winter
Hister (2) = Danube River
ille = that river
marmareus, a, um = marbled
meminit = remembers (this word usually
takes the genitive case)
Nasonis = genitive of Naso (which is one
of my names)
-ne = attached to the first word in a
sentence to indicate a question
premo (3) = I crush
repello (3) = I fend off
tepeo (2) = I am warm

You might notice that there are two words, which look very similar, and mean something very similar, which are "hac" and "has". It's about time I introduced you to this very common set of words. It's something called a 'demonstrative pronoun', which is a way of saying that you are using word in a way that is similar to pointing – "these ones here". As you already know, the word changes to agree with what it is describing, so you saw:

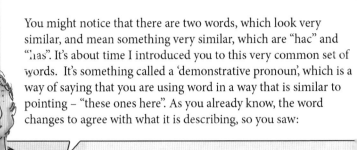

tremens caelum **has**
gentes premit.
The trembling sky
crushes **these tribes**.

And:

ego **in hac**
barbaria habito
I am living **in**
this barbarity.

Here is how this volatile word behaves:

	MASCULINE	FEMININE	NEUTER
Nom.	hic (this)	haec	hoc
Acc.	hunc	hanc	hoc
Gen.	huius	huius	huius
Dat.	huic	huic	huic
Abl.	hoc	hac	hoc
Nom. pl.	hi (these)	hae	haec
Acc. pl.	hos	has	haec
Gen. pl.	horum	harum	horum
Dat. pl.	his	his	his
Abl. pl.	his	his	his

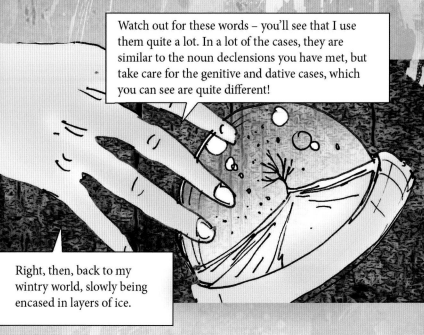

Watch out for these words – you'll see that I use them quite a lot. In a lot of the cases, they are similar to the noun declensions you have met, but take care for the genitive and dative cases, which you can see are quite different!

Right, then, back to my wintry world, slowly being encased in layers of ice.

nix iacet. sol imberque non resolvunt. Boreas illam indurat perpetuamque facit.
ergo ubi prima nix nondum delicuit, altera nix venit!
in multis locis nix duos annos manere solet.
pellibus et bracis Tomitae mala frigora arcent.
vultus solus de toto corpore patet. saepe capilli glacie pendente sonant.
barba gelu nitet.

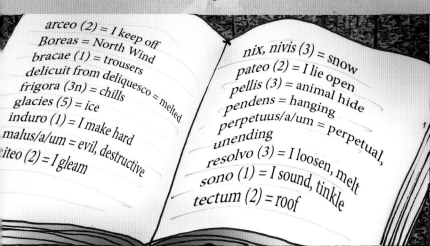

arceo (2) = I keep off
Boreas = North Wind
bracae (1) = trousers
delicuit from deliquesco = melted
frigora (3n) = chills
glacies (5) = ice
induro (1) = I make hard
malus/a/um = evil, destructive
iteo (2) = I gleam

nix, nivis (3) = snow
pateo (2) = I lie open
pellis (3) = animal hide
pendens = hanging
perpetuus/a/um = perpetual, unending
resolvo (3) = I loosen, melt
sono (1) = I sound, tinkle
tectum (2) = roof

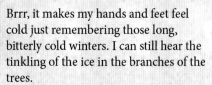

Brrr, it makes my hands and feet feel cold just remembering those long, bitterly cold winters. I can still hear the tinkling of the ice in the branches of the trees.

I have another of those pointy pronouns to show you – you have met it from time to time before, and there was even one in that last passage. It is our friend 'ille, illa, illud' meaning 'that' or in the plural, 'those', and this is how it goes.

	MASCULINE	FEMININE	NEUTER
Nom.	ille	illa	illud
Acc.	illum	illam	illud
Gen.	illius	illius	illius
Dat.	illi	illi	illi
Abl.	illo	illa	illo
Nom. pl.	illi	illae	illa
Acc. pl.	illos	illas	illa
Gen. pl.	illorum	illarum	illorum
Dat. pl.	illis	illis	illis
Abl. pl.	illis	illis	illis

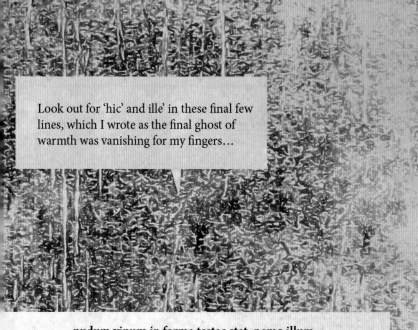

Look out for 'hic' and ille' in these final few lines, which I wrote as the final ghost of warmth was vanishing for my fingers...

nudum vinum in forma testae stat. nemo illum fundere potest. Tomitae frusta bibunt. rivi hoc gelu concrescunt. de lacu Tomitae fragiles aquas effodiunt. Hister ipse suas caeruleas aquas congelat. rivus in mare tectis aquis serpit.

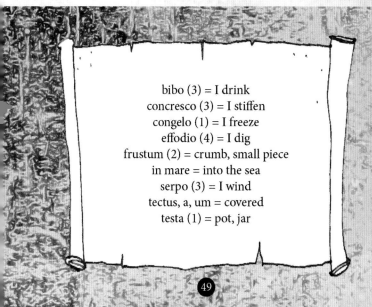

bibo (3) = I drink
concresco (3) = I stiffen
congelo (1) = I freeze
effodio (4) = I dig
frustum (2) = crumb, small piece
in mare = into the sea
serpo (3) = I wind
tectus, a, um = covered
testa (1) = pot, jar

Activities

Do you remember in my last book that the world got flooded and everything changed in new and strange ways? Trees flowed in mighty rivers, and lions swam in the seas. You might notice something similar about this story – except this isn't a story.

You've probably walked on frozen streams and heard the eerie tinkling of branches encased in ice gently knocking each other in the freezing breeze. Can you tell a story of a natural event – like the spring when plants start to emerge – and focus on the sense of magical transformation?

There are different words for 'cold' and 'ice' and 'freezing' in this passage – perhaps you can pick them out. How might you translate them in ways that make the words different and interesting?

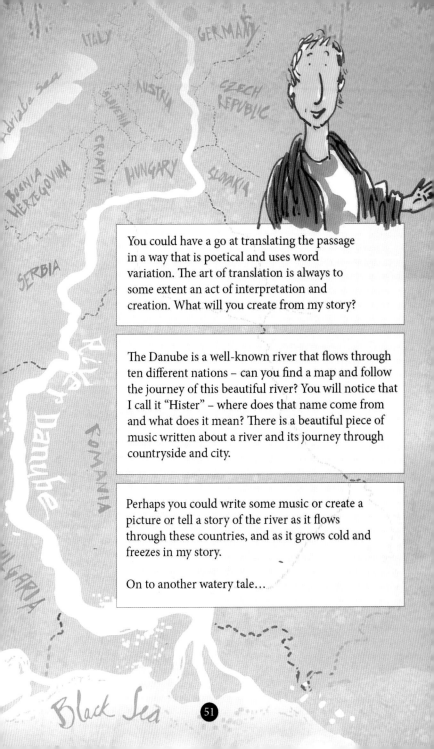

You could have a go at translating the passage in a way that is poetical and uses word variation. The art of translation is always to some extent an act of interpretation and creation. What will you create from my story?

The Danube is a well-known river that flows through ten different nations – can you find a map and follow the journey of this beautiful river? You will notice that I call it "Hister" – where does that name come from and what does it mean? There is a beautiful piece of music written about a river and its journey through countryside and city.

Perhaps you could write some music or create a picture or tell a story of the river as it flows through these countries, and as it grows cold and freezes in my story.

On to another watery tale…

Cyane

Eventually those long and seemingly endless winters would begin to come to an end, and the first sign would be that a first thick layer of ice would start to melt. When this happened, I would often find myself thinking of Cyane, a goddess of a spring. It all happened because Pluto had seen the beautiful daughter of Proserpina out picking flowers in the fields. He snatched her into his black chariot and swept her away, but Cyane saw them.

Cyane gurgite medio, tenus alvo, exstitit. illa deum agnovit et
'noli longius ire!' clamavit.
'invitae Cereris gener esse non potes: roga puellam, non carpe!'.
dixit, et tendens bracchia, in diversas partes obstitit.
Pluto non iram tenuit.
hortans suos terribiles equos, in ima gurgitis sceptrum condidit.
icta terra viam in Tartarum fecit, et currum medio cratere
recepit.

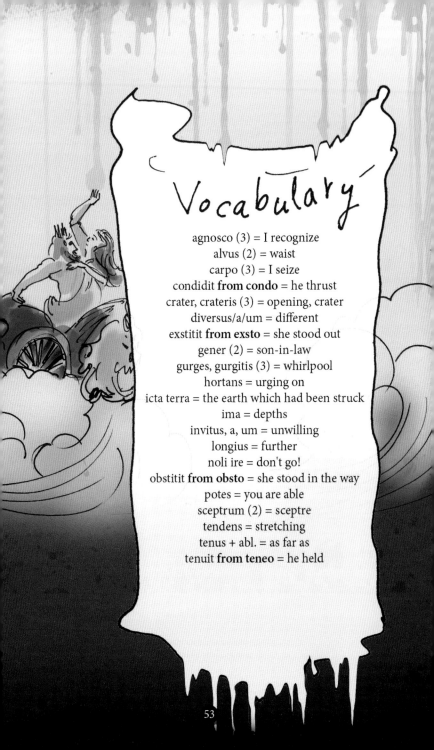

Vocabulary

agnosco (3) = I recognize
alvus (2) = waist
carpo (3) = I seize
condidit **from condo** = he thrust
crater, crateris (3) = opening, crater
diversus/a/um = different
exstitit **from exsto** = she stood out
gener (2) = son-in-law
gurges, gurgitis (3) = whirlpool
hortans = urging on
icta terra = the earth which had been struck
ima = depths
invitus, a, um = unwilling
longius = further
noli ire = don't go!
obstitit **from obsto** = she stood in the way
potes = you are able
sceptrum (2) = sceptre
tendens = stretching
tenus + abl. = as far as
tenuit **from teneo** = he held

Look at the words 'tendens' and 'hortans' – what do you notice about how they are used? They describe an action, 'stretching', 'encouraging', that is going on at the same time as the main verb.

This way of using the verb is called the 'present participle', and it is using a verb as an adjective. Like adjectives, the words agree – in this case with the person who is doing the action. For example:

Cyane tendens bracchia obstitit.
Cyane stretching her arms, stood in the way.

Pluto deam tendentem bracchia vidit.
Pluto saw the goddess stretching out her arms.

This is how the present participle declines – like a third declension noun:

	GROUP 1	GROUP 2	GROUP 3	GROUP 4
Nom.	amans	monens	mittens	audiens
Acc.	amantem	monentem	mittentem	audientem
Gen.	amantis	monentis	mittentis	audientis
Dat.	amanti	monenti	mittenti	audienti
Abl.	amante	monente	mittente	audiente
Nom. pl.	amantes	monentes	mittentes	audientes
Acc. pl.	amantes	monentes	mittentes	audientes
Gen. pl.	amantium	monentium	mittentium	audientium
Dat. pl.	amantibus	monentibus	mittentibus	audientibus
Abl. pl.	amantibus	monentibus	mittentibus	audientibus

Let's move onto the next part of Cyane's story.

55

Cyane raptam deam suumque fontem maeret.
inconsolabile vulnus mente tacita gerit. lacrimis absumitur.
membra molliunt, ossa flectunt, ungues rigorem ponunt.
prima tenuissima liquescunt: caerulei capilli digitique et crura pedesque.
post haec, umeri tergumque latusque pectusque in tenues rivos abeunt.
denique pro sanguine lympha venas subit.
restat nihil, quod prendere potes.

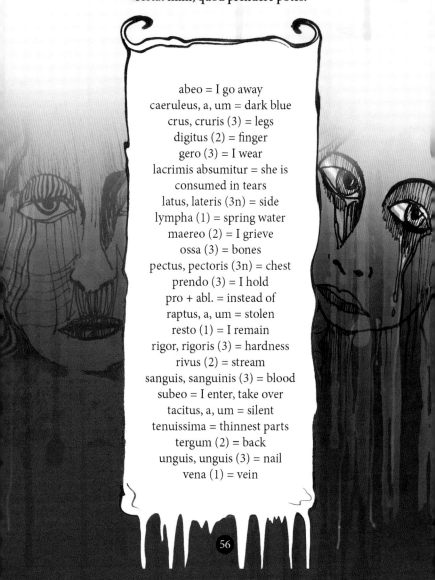

abeo = I go away
caeruleus, a, um = dark blue
crus, cruris (3) = legs
digitus (2) = finger
gero (3) = I wear
lacrimis absumitur = she is
consumed in tears
latus, lateris (3n) = side
lympha (1) = spring water
maereo (2) = I grieve
ossa (3) = bones
pectus, pectoris (3n) = chest
prendo (3) = I hold
pro + abl. = instead of
raptus, a, um = stolen
resto (1) = I remain
rigor, rigoris (3) = hardness
rivus (2) = stream
sanguis, sanguinis (3) = blood
subeo = I enter, take over
tacitus, a, um = silent
tenuissima = thinnest parts
tergum (2) = back
unguis, unguis (3) = nail
vena (1) = vein

Activities

That's quite a story – a girl that literally melts into tears.

We all use the expression, and in this story, the expression becomes real. Can you think of any other expressions which might be made real?

Perhaps you could write a story about it, a bit like my little story.

The thing I enjoyed telling most in this tale is the minute little details – how the delicate bits like her nails were the first to melt, and then the rest of her followed, until finally her veins flowed with water. It would make a beautiful watery painting…

But did you notice something about the colour of her hair even before the transformation? Another clue is in her name – Cyane – have you seen that word used before? In so many of these stories there are little pointers, hinting at the direction of the story.

You can think of them like sign-posts – if you recall the plot of some of your favourite stories, can you spot the signs telling the reader which direction the story is heading? You could create a comic strip illustration of the story with actual sign-posts here and there in the images!

Let's carry on, as there are still a few stories left before our final farewell.

chapter septem

Ver

Cyane melted into water; and so at last did the stiff ice of winter at Tomi. Have you ever noticed those first traces of warmth beginning to return after a long, cold winter? It can feel quite magical. Here in Tomi, too, I began to see those early signs that the deep cold was starting to lose its hold over the landscape.

iam Zephyri frigora minuunt.
iam pueri hilaresque puellae violas legunt.
prata floribus variorum colorum pubescunt.
loquaces aves canunt, et hirundo sub trabibus cunas facit.
herba, quae sub sulcis latuit, exit.
tum cacumen molle humo expandit.

Vocabulary

cacumen, cacuminis (3n) = tip

cunae (1) = nest (this Latin word is plural in form, but singular in meaning)

expando (3) = I spread out

floribus **from flos** = with flowers

herba (1) = grass

hirundo, hirundinis (3) = swallow

hilaris/e = cheerful

latuit **from lateo** = it lay hidden

lego (3) = I pick

loquax, loquacis = talkative

minuo (3) = I lessen

pubesco (3) = I ripen

pratum (2) = meadow

trabs. trabis (3) = beam

sulcus (2) = furrow

viola (1) = violet

Zephyrus (2) = a gentle west wind

Before we go any further, it's time to introduce you to some new grammar. Have a look at this line, which you have just translated:

herba, quae sub sulcis latuit, exit.

"The grass, which lay hidden under the furrows, emerges".

61

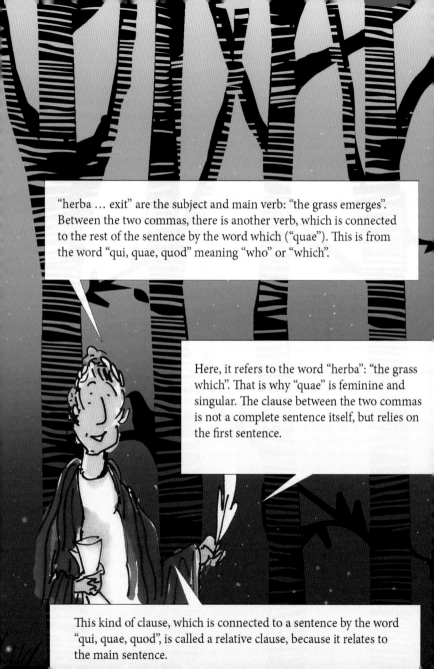

"herba … exit" are the subject and main verb: "the grass emerges". Between the two commas, there is another verb, which is connected to the rest of the sentence by the word which ("quae"). This is from the word "qui, quae, quod" meaning "who" or "which".

Here, it refers to the word "herba": "the grass which". That is why "quae" is feminine and singular. The clause between the two commas is not a complete sentence itself, but relies on the first sentence.

This kind of clause, which is connected to a sentence by the word "qui, quae, quod", is called a relative clause, because it relates to the main sentence.

Here is another example from the story of Cyane, which you may remember from last time:

restat nihil, quod prendere potes.

"Nothing remains, which you are able to hold".

The relative clause has been put into italics, so you can see how the clause is introduced by a form of the word "qui, quae, quod". The word "which" ("quod") here refers to "nihil". That is why it is neuter singular, because nihil is a neuter noun.

We'll do some more on relative clauses. For now, just try to recognise them and translate them. Here are those important endings for **qui, quae, quod!**

Nom.	qui	quae	quod
Acc.	quem	quam	quod
Gen.	cuius	cuius	cuius
Dat.	cui	cui	cui
Abl.	quo	quo	quo
Nom. pl.	qui	quae	quae
Acc. pl.	quos	quas	quae
Gen. pl.	quorum	quarum	quorum
Dat. pl.	quibus	quibus	quibus
Abl. pl.	quibus	quibus	quibus

Back to the beautiful arrival of spring!

sol vernus nivem solvit. viri aquas duras lacu non fodiunt.
mare glacie non concrescit. nec, ut ante, per Histrum
stridula plaustra bubulcus agit.
aliquae naves huc adnare incipiunt, quas sedulus saluto.
"unde venis? cur venis? quis es?" rogo.
quisquis vir est, rumorem et triumphos Caesaris narrare potest.

adnare **from adno** = to sail towards
bubulcus (2) = ploughman
concresco (3) = I stiffen
fodio (4) = I dig
huc = to here
narrare **from narro** = to tell of
nec = nor
per = over
potest **from possum** = he is able
plaustrum (2) = wagon
quis? = who?
quisquis = whoever
rumor, rumoris (3) = news
saluto (1) = I greet
sedulus/a/um = eager
stridulus/a/um = creaking
triumphus (2) = triumph
unde = from where?
vernus/a/um = of spring

Have you spotted the relative clause in the second part of my story?

Here it is:

aliquae naves huc adnare incipiunt, **quas sedulus saluto.**

"Some ships begin to sail here, which I greet eagerly."

Do you see how "quas" connects the clause to the main sentence, referring to the ships which are the subject of the main clause? You might notice, though, that "quas" is accusative, whereas "naves" is nominative.

This is because the relative pronoun takes its **number** (plural) and **gender** (feminine) from the noun it is connected to.

However, it takes its **case** (accusative) from its position within the relative clause.

While the ships are the subject of the main clause (they "begin to sail"), they are actually the object of the relative clause (I greet **them** eagerly).

We'll see some more relative clauses in my final chapter!

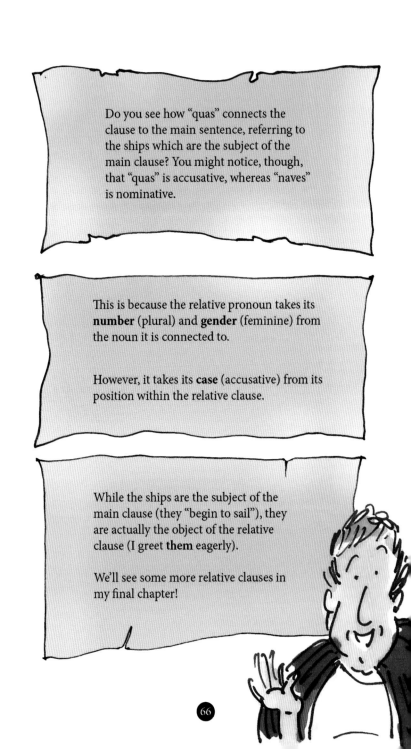

Activities

As you can tell from the story, one of the things that I most loved about the spring was the ships that would appear on the horizon, bringing precious bits of news about the rest of the world. I would lap up every detail!

Can you imagine a story told by one of the many sailors I met – what amazing things had they seen, and what places were they journeying to? What news might they have brought from **Roma**?

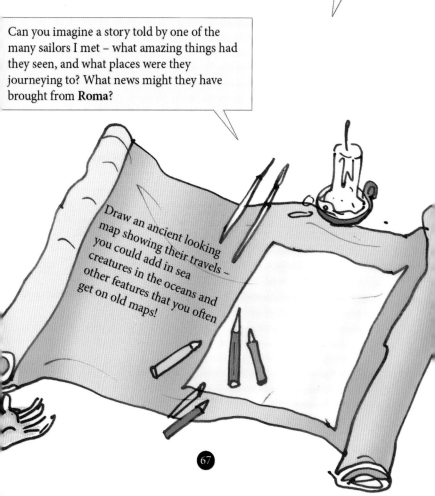

Draw an ancient looking map showing their travels – you could add in sea creatures in the oceans and other features that you often get on old maps!

Spring is so magical! Even though in your time you might now understand the causes of each process of life reawakening, I'm sure nothing can diminish the feeling of some sort of special elixir that is bringing everything to life! Can you choose an aspect of the arrival of spring but describe it in a way that makes the process seem magical?

We often associate spring with bird song, and different birds are mentioned in my story – can you remember them? Below is a list of other Latin names for birds, as well as list of verbs for the sound they make. Can you work out which bird makes which sound?

Birds	Verbs for bird sounds
anaticula	tutabat
corvus	grocat
avicula	tetrinnit
noctua	pipit
alauda	

Pygmalion

We are almost at the end
of our time together. I
hope you have enjoyed the
many magical stories
we've explored, as well as
the tale of my journeys to
distant lands. Before you
go, I have one more story
for you. It's a story that is
especially close to my
heart, as it is all about the
transformational power of
the imagination to bring
things to life. It is the tale
of the sculptor Pygmalion.

Pygmalion sine uxore caelebs vivebat.
interea niveum ebur mira arte sculpsit.
formam fecit, quam nulla femina habebat.
tum formae amorem concepit.
facies erat verae feminae, quam vivere credas.
formam movere credas. Pygmalion stupebat.
saepe formam manibus tangebat. eratne
corpus an ebur? Pygmalion non certus erat.

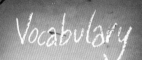

Vocabulary

amorem concepit = "he fell in love"
an = or
ars, artis (3) = art, skill
caelebs = on his own
certus/a/um = certain
credas = "you would believe"
ebur, eboris (3n) = ivory
facies (5) = face
forma (1) = shape, form
interea = meanwhile
mirus/a/um = wondrous
sculpo (3) = I carve
uxor, uxoris (3) = wife
verus/a/um = real, true

Did you spot the relative clauses in the first part of my story? There are two of them to find.

Here they are:

formam fecit, **quam nulla femina habebat.**
'He made a shape, which no woman had.'

facies erat verae feminae, **quam vivere credas.**
It was the face of a real woman, who seemed
to be living.

In both examples, the relative pronoun 'quam' is accusative,
singular and feminine. In the first example, 'quam' refers to 'forma'
which is singular and feminine, and in example two, it refers to
'femina', which is also singular and feminine. In the relative clause
itself (which I have put in bold), the pronoun is the object in both
clauses, which is why they are both 'quam'.

Pygmalion has fallen in love with his own statue. Have you ever fallen in love with something you've created? Perhaps it was a story you spent a long time writing or something you made or built or drew? I know I have. Let's see what happens next.

Pygmalion oscula formae dabat. formae dicebat,
et formam esse veram feminam credebat.
munera ferebat: conchas et teretes lapillos
et parvas aves et flores mille colorum.
lilia et pilas et Heliadum lacrimas ferebat.
digitis gemmas dabat, et longa monilia collo dabat.
aure leves bacae pendebant, et pectore redimicula pendebant.

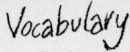

Vocabulary

aure = 'from her ear'
baca (1) = pearl
concha (1) = oyster shell
gemma (1) = gem
Heliadum lacrimas = 'tears of the Heliades'
(i.e. amber)
lapillus (2) = little stone
lilium (2) = lily
mille = thousand
monilia (3n) = necklaces
munera (3n) = gifts
osculum (2) = kiss
pectore = 'from her chest'
pendo (3) = I hang
pila (1) = mortar (bowl for crushing up herbs)
redimicula (2n) = bands
teres, teretis = smooth, polished

Pygmalion cannot believe that his statue is not real!
He tends to it as if it were living person, bringing it
gifts, talking to it, and longing for it to respond.
What do you think will happen next?

festa dies Veneris venit!
Pygmalion dixit "si, dei, dare omnia potestis, da mihi uxorem!".
Venus audivit. cum Pygmalion rediit, oscula formae dedit.
forma erat tepida!
manibus quoque formam temptavit.
ebur mollescit, sicut cera sole mollescit.
corpus erat! venae saliunt.
femina oscula sensit et erubuit.
timidos oculos attollens, femina Pygmalion vidit.

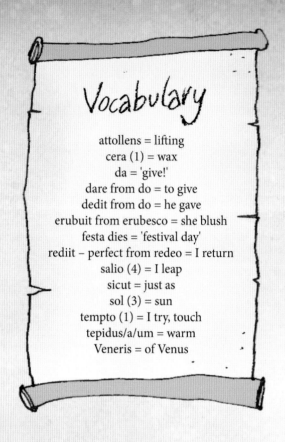

Vocabulary

attollens = lifting
cera (1) = wax
da = 'give!'
dare from do = to give
dedit from do = he gave
erubuit from erubesco = she blush
festa dies = 'festival day'
rediit – perfect from redeo = I return
salio (4) = I leap
sicut = just as
sol (3) = sun
tempto (1) = I try, touch
tepidus/a/um = warm
Veneris = of Venus

We'll leave that story there for now. Does Pygmalion get his happy ending? What will become of his living creation – will the woman fall in love with him or will she want to leave?

These are all things you can imagine. Whenever you create something, it takes on a life of its own and this causes things to happen that you might never have predicted or thought possible. That's certainly what I've found.

I hope you've enjoyed this journey. Here I must leave you for the final time, but if you ever want to find me again, you can read my many poems, where you will find other journeys, and more magical happenings.

Perhaps you can create your own ending to the story I've been telling in this final chapter. What will happen to the woman formed from the statue? How does the world seem to her? What will she do? If it happened today, imagine the reaction from the media, from scientists, and from everyone else! There are so many possibilities to explore....

Vale.

Vocabulary

A

abfuerunt from absum = they were far away
abeo = I go away
absum = I am absent/away
accensus/a/um = burnt
accepit from accipio = he accepted
accipio (3) = I accept, receive
acer (2) = maple tree
acerbus/a/um = bitter, gloomy
ad = at, to
addo (3) = I add
ademptus/a/um = banished
adhuc = still
adno (1) = I sail
adopertus/a/um = covered
adsum = I am here
advenio (4) = I arrive at, meet
aedificavit from aedifico = he built
aedifico (1) = I build
aeneus/a/um = bronze
aequor (3) = sea
aer, aeris (3) = air
aetas, aetatis (3) = age
aestas, aestatis (3) = summer
aeternus/a/um = eternal
ager (2) = field
agnosco (3) = I recognise
ago (3) = I do, drive
ala (1) = wing
alauda (1) = lark
albus/a = white
alterus/a = other
altissimus/a = highest
alvus (2) = waist
amo (1) = I love
amicus (2) = friend
amor, amoris (3) = love
an = or
ancilla (1) = slave-girl

anaticula (1) = duck
antrum (2) = cave
anus (2) = old woman
appareo (2) = I appear
aqua (1) = water
aranea (1) = spider
arator (3) = ploughman
arbor, arboris (3) = tree
arceo (2) = I keep off
ardeo (2) = I burn
arduus/a/um = steep
argenteus/a/um = silver
ars, artis (3) = skill
ascenderunt from ascendo = they climbed
ascendo (3) = I climb
aspicio (3) = I look at
ater/atra/atrum = black
atque = and
attollens = lifting
audio (4) = I hear
aufero = I steal, take away
augustus/a/um = majestic
aura (1) = breeze
aureus/a/um = gold
aures (3) = ears
Aurora (1) = the goddess Dawn
autumnus (2) = autumn
avicula (1) = little bird
avidus/a/um = greedy
avis, avis (3) = bird
axis, axis (3) = axle

B

baca (1) = pearl
baculum (2) = stick
barba (1) = beard
barbaria (1) = barbarity
bellum (2) = war
blanditiae (1) = sweet words

bonus/a/um = good
bracae (1) = trousers
brevis/e = short
bubulcus (2) = ploughman
buxum (2) = box tree

C

cacumen, cacuminis (3n) = tip
cado (3) = I fall
caelebs = unmarried, single
caelum (2) = sky
caeruleus, a, um = dark blue
callidus/a/um = crafty
calor, caloris (3) = heat
candidus/a/um = gleaming white
canis, canis (3) = dog
cantavit from canto = he sang
canto (1) = I sing
capillae (1) = hair
captavit from capto = he captured
capto (1) = I capture
caput, capitis (3) = head
carmen, carminis (3) = song
carpserunt from carpo = they seized
carpo = I seize
carus/a/um = dear
causa (1) = reason
cave = beware!
caverna (1) = cave
cecidit from cado = he fell
cedo (3) = I concede
celo (1) = I hide
cena (1) = dinner
cera (1) = wax
certus/a/um = certain
ceterus/a/um = the rest
cibum (2) = food
cinis, cineris (3) = ash
clamo (1) = I shout

clamor, clamoris (3) = shout
collis, collis (3) = hill
communis/e = communal
concha (1) = oyster shell
concresco (3) = I stiffen
condidit from condo = he thrust
condo (3) = I thrust
congelo (1) = I freeze
congero (3) = I pile up, gather
congerunt from congero = they piled up
coniunx, coniugis (3) = wife/husband
coniuro (1) = I plot
consilium (2) = advice
constituo (3) = I set up, decide
consumo (3) = I eat
contiguus/a/um = neighbouring
convaleo (2) = I recover
corvus (2) = crow
corpus, corporis (3) = body
corylus (2) = hazel tree
crater, crateris (3) = opening, crater
creavit from creo = he created
creo (1) = I create
crescentes = growing
cresco (3) = I grow
crevit from cresco = it grew
croceus/a/um = yellow
crus, cruris (3n) = leg
cum = with
cunae (1) = nest
cupio (4) = I desire
cur = why?
curro (3) = I run
currus (4) = chariot
custos, custodis (3) = guard

D

de = down from
dea (1) = goddess

dedit from do = he gave
deinde = then
deleo (2) = I destroy
delicuit from deliquesco = it melted
deliquesco (3) = I melt
demitto (3) = I thrust
dens, dentis (3) = tooth
densus/a/um = dense
descendo (3) = I descend
dico (3) = I say
digitus (2) = finger
diligenter = carefully
discedo (3) = I go away
diu = for a long time
do (1) = I give
doceo (2) = I teach
domina (1)= mistress
dominus (2) = master
domus (4) = house, home
donec = until
donum (2) = gift
duas = two
duco (3) = I lead
duxit from duco = he led

E

ebur, eboris (3n) = ivory
ecce! = look!
effodio (4) = I dig
ego = I
emitto (3) = I send out
enumero (1) = I count
equus (2) = horse
erat from sum = was
error, erroris (3) = error
erubesco (3) = I blush, redden
erubuit from erubesco = she reddened
et = and

evanesco (3) = I vanish
exclamavit from exclamo = he called out
exclamo (1) = I call out
expando (3) = I spread out
exstitit from exsto = she stood out
exsto (3) = I stand out
extremus/a/um = far, extreme
exilium (2) = exile
exspecto (1) = I wait for
exululo (1) = I howl

F

facies (5) = face
facio (3) = I do, make
fagus (2) = beech tree
fallo (3) = I deceive
falsus/a/um = false
fama (1) = fame
fatum (2) = fate
femina (1) = woman
fenestra (1) = window
fer = bring!
feritas, feritatis (3) = ferocity
ferreus/a/um = iron
fessus/a /um= tired
festino (1) = I hurry
fio = I become
figo (3) = I strike
filia (1) = daughter
filius (2) = son
filum (2) = thread
finio (4) = I finish
finis, finis (3) = end
finivit from finio = he finished
flamma (1) = flame
flecto (3) = I turn, bend
flexit from flecto = he turned
flos, floris (3) = flower
fluo (3) = I flow

folium (2) = leaf, petal
forma (1) = shape
fortis/e = brave
fraxinus (2) = ash tree
frigidus/a/um = cold
frigora (3n) = chills
frons, frondis (3) = leaf
frustra = in vain
frustum (2) = crumb, small piece
fulmen, fulminis (3) = thunderbolt
fundo (3) = I pour
fusus (2) = spindle

G

gaudeo (2) = I enjoy
gelu, gelus (3n) = ice
gemma (1) = gem
gener (2) = son-in-law
gens, gentis (3) = people
gero (3) = I wear
glacies (5) = ice
gladius (2) = sword
glomero (1) = I gather together
gravis/e = heavy
grex, gregis (3) = flock
gurges, gurgitis (3) = whirlpool
gutta (1) = tear

H

habenae (1) = reins
habeo (2) = I have
habito (1) = I live
haereo (2) = I stick
herba (1) = grass
hic/haec/hoc = this
hic = here
hiems, hiemis (3) = winter
hilaris/e = cheerful

hirundo, hirundinis (3) = swallow
hodie = today
hortans = urging on
hortus (2) = garden
humus (2) = ground
huc = to here

I

iacite = throw!
iacio (3/4) = I throw
iam = now
ianua (1) = door
ibi = there
idem/eadem/idem = the same
iecur (3) = liver
igitur = therefore
ignis, ignis (3) = fire
ilia (2) = insides
ille/illa/illud = he/she/that
ima = depths
imago, imaginis (3) = image
imber, imbris (3) = rain
impelo (3) = I drive
in = in/on
induro (1) = I make hard
incipio (4) = I begin
infirmus/a/um = shaky
initium (2) = beginning
innumerus/a/um = countless
inquit = he/she says
intendens = stretching
interea = meanwhile
intra = inside
intravit from intro = he entered
intro (1) = I enter
invenio (4) = I find
invenit from invenio = he found
invito (1) = I invite
invitus/a/um = unwilling

ipsus/a/um = himself/herself/itself
iratus/a/um = angry
iratissimus/a/um = very angry
ita = in this way
ita vero = yes
iter, itineris (3) = journey
iterum = again
iubeo (2) = I order
iugulum (2) = throat
Iuppiter, Iovis (3) = Jupiter
iussit from iubeo = he ordered
iuvenis, iuvenis (3) = young man

L

labor. laboris (3) = work
labyrinthus (2) = maze
lacertus (2) = arm
lacrimo (1) = I cry
laetus/a/um = happy
lana (1) = wool
lapillus (2) = little stone
lapis, lapidis (3) = stone
lateo (2) = I hide
latuit from lateo = it lay hidden
latus, lateris (3n) = side
laudo (1) = I praise
laurus (2) = laurel tree
lego (3)= I pick
leo, leonis (3) = lion
lex, legis (3) = rule
ligavit from ligo = he tied
ligo (1) = I tie, bind
lilium (2) = lily
liquidus/a = clear
litus, litoris (3n) = shore
locus (2) = place
longius = further
longus/a/um = long
loquax = talkative

luceo (2) = I gleam
ludo (3) = I play
luna (1) = moon
lupus (2) = wolf
lux, lucis (3) = light
lympha (1) = spring water

M

Maeandrus (2) = the river Maeander
maereo (2) = I grieve
magister (2) = teacher
magnus/a/um = large
malus/a/um = evil
maneo (2) = I stay
marmareus/a/um = marble
mater, matris (3) = mother
medius/a/um = middle
membrum (2) = limb
memorabilis/e = memorable
mensa (1) = table
mercator, mercatoris (3) = merchant
meus/a/um = my
mihi = to/for me
mille = yhousand
minimus/a/um = very small
minuo (3) = I lessen
mirabilis/e = wonderful
mirus/a/um = wondrous
misceo (2) = I mix
mitto (3) = I send
modo = only
moles, molis (3) = mass
mollio (4) = I soften
moneo (2) = I warn, advise
monilia (3n) = necklaces
mons, montis (3) = mountain
mora (1) = delay
moveo (2) = I move
movit from moveo = he moved

mox = soon
multus/a/um = many
murus (2) = wall
muto (1) = I change
myrtus (2) = myrtle tree

N

narro (1) = I tell of
naso (3) = nose
nato (1) = I swim
natura (1) = nature
navis (3) = ship
nec = nor
necesse = necessary
nego (1) = I deny
Nereis = sea nymph
nervus (2) = string
nescio (4) = I do not know
niger, nigra, nigrum = black
nil = nothing
nisi = except
niteo (2) = I bleam
niveus/a/um = snow-white
nix, nivis (3) = snow
noctua (1) = owl
noli = don't
nomen, nominis (3) = name
non = not
nos = we
nota (1) = sign
notitia (1) = notice
Notus (2) = South wind
novus/a/um = new
nubes, nubis (3) = cloud
nudus/a/um = bare
nullus/a/um = no
nupta (1) = bride
nunc = now
nympha (1) = nymph

O

obruo (3) = I rush against
obscurus/a/um = obscure
observo (1) = I watch
obsto (1) = I stand in the way
occido (3) = I die
oceanus (2) = ocean
oculus (2) = eye
oderat from odi = he hated
odi = I hate
olim = once
omnis/e = all
opis, opis (3) = help
orbis, orbis (3) = globe, ball
ordo, ordinis (3) = order
oro (1) = I beg, pray
osculum (2) = kiss
ossa (3) = bones

P

paene = almost
palleo (2) = I grow pale
paro (1) = I prepare
parvus/a/um = small
pastor, pastoris (3) = shepherd
pateo (2) = I lie open
pater (3) = father
paulatim = little by little
pectus, pectoris (3) = chest
pecunia (1) = money
pecus, pecudis (3) = flock
pellis, pellis (3) = animal hide
pello (3) = I strike
pes, pedis (3) = foot
pendens = hanging
pendo (3) = I hang
penna (1) = feather

percutio (3) = I hit
periculosus/a/um = dangerous
perpetuus/a/um = perpetual, unending
perterritus/a/um = terrified
pervenio (4) = I reach
pharetra (1) = quiver
pila (1) = mortar
pingo (3) = I create a picture of
piscis, piscis (3) = fish
platanus (2) = plane tree
plaustrum (2) = wagon
plumbeus/a/um = lead
pomum (2) = fruit
pono (3) = I put, place
porto (1) = I carry
post = after
postquam = after
posuit from pono = he put
poterant from possum = they were able
poterat from possum = he was able
praeceps = headlong
pratum (2) = meadow
premo (3) = I crush
prendo (3) = I hold
primus/a/um = first
prius = before
pro + abl. = instead of
probo (1) = I prove
procul = far away
pronus/a/um = facing downwards
pubesco (3) = I ripen
puella (1) = girl
puer (2) = boy
pugno (1) = I fight
pulcherrimus/a/um = very beautiful, most
beautiful

Q

quaerens = seeking

quaereo (2) = I seek
qualis = just like
quamvis = although
quantus/a/um = how great
quartus/a/um = fourth
quassatus/a/um = shaken
quatio (4) = I shake
qui/quae/quod = who, which
quid = what?
quis = who?
quisquis = whoever
quod = because
quoque = also

R

radius (2) = spoke (of wheel)
radix, radicis (3) = root
ramus (2) = branch
rapio (3) = I seize
raptus/a/um = stolen
recentes = recent
redeo = I return
redimicula (2) = bands
rediit from redeo = he returned
refluo (3) = I flow back
regia (1) = palace
resolvo (3) = I loosen
rex, regis (3) = the king
relabor (1) = I fall back
relapsa est from relabor = she fell back
relinquo (3) = I leave
removeo (2) = I remove
repello (3) = I fend off
repeto (3) = I repeat, call
respondo (3) = I reply
resto (1) = I remain
retego (3) = I unravel
retro = backwards
reverto (3) = I return, turn back

rideo (2) = I laugh
rigor, rigoris (3) = hardness
rima (1) = crack
ripa (1) = riverbank
ripuit from rapio = she seized
rivus (2) = river, stream
rogo (1) = I ask
rota (1) = wheel
rudis/e = rough
rumor, rumoris (3) = news
rus, ruris (3n) = countryside

S

saeculum (2) = age, time
saepe = often
sagitta (1) = arrow
salio (4) = I leap
salix (2) = willow tree
saluto (1) = I greet
sanguis, sanguinis (3) = blood
scelus, sceleris (3n) = crime
sceptrum (2) = sceptre
scindo (3) = I cut
scio (4) = I know
scopulum (2) = rock
scribo (3) = I write
sculpo (3) = I sculpt
secundus/a/um = second
sed = but
sedeo (2) = I sit
sedit from sedeo = he sat
sedulus/a/um = eager
semper = always
sensus (4) = sense
separo (1) = I separate
serius = later
serpens, serpentis (3) = snake
servus (2) = slave
servo (1) = I keep

sibi = to/for him
silentium (2) = silence
silva (1) = wood
simulo (1) = I pretend to be
sino (3) = I allow
sol = sun
solus/a = alone
sollicitus/a = worried
sono (1) = I sound
spargo (3) = I scatter
spectavit from specto = she looked at
specto (1) = I look at
sperno (3) = I reject
stamen, staminis (3) = thread
statim = straightaway
stella (1) = star
stipuit from stupeo = he was dumbfounded
stipuerunt from stupeo = they were dumbfounded
sto (1) = I stand
stridulus/a/um = creaking
stultus/a/um = stupid
stupeo (2) = I am dumbfounded
Stygius/a/um = of the River Styx
sub + abl. = under
subeo = I emerge, enter, take over
subit from subeo = it emerged, entered, took
over
subito = suddenly
subsido (3) = I subside
subter = underneath
sulcus (2) = furrow
sum = I am
summus/a,/um = highest, topmost
superbia (1) = pride
supersum = I survive, remain
supremus/a/um = final
suus/a/um = his, her, its

T

taberna (1) = shop
tabesco (2) = I melt
tacitus/a/um = silent
tamen = however
tandem = at last
tango (3) = I touch
tardus/a/um = slow
tectum (2) = roof
tectus/a/um = covered
tego (3) = I weave
tela (1) = loom
temerarius/a/um = rash
temo. temonis (3) = pole
templum (2) = temple
tempto (1) = I try, touch
tempus, temporis (3) = time
tendens = stretching
teneo (2) = I hold
tenuis/e = thin
tenuissima = thinnest parts
tenus + abl. = as far as
tepeo (2) = I am warm
tepidus/a/um = warm
teres = smooth, polished
tergum (2) = back
terra (1) = land
tertius/a/um = third
testa (1) = pot, jar
tibi = to/for you
timeo (2) = I am afraid
tollo (3) = I lift up
torreo (2) = I bake
tot = so many
trabs, trabis (3) = beam
tristis/e = sad
triumphus (2) = triumph
tu = you
tum = then
tumulus (2) = tomb
turbavit from turbo = he mixed up
turbo (1) = I disturb, mix up
turris, turris (3) = tower

U

uber = rich, fruitful
ubi = when/where
ubique = on all sides
ullus/a /um= any
ultimus/a/um = last
umbra (1) = shadow, ghost
unguis, unguis (3) = nail
unde = from where?
unus/una = one
urbs, urbis (3) = city
usus (4) = loan
utrum = each
uxor, uxoris (3) = wife

V

vallis, vallis (3) = valley
vatis, vatis (3) = poet
velamen, velaminis (3n) = veil
velut = just as
vena (1) = vein
venio (3) = I come
venter, ventris (3) = stomach
ver, veris (3n) = spring
verbum (2) = word
vernus/a/um = of spring
verto (3) = I turn
verus/a/um = true
vestigium (2) = trace
vestis (3) = clothes
vetuerunt from veto = they forbade
veto (1) = I forbid

vetus = old
via (1) = path
vicinia (1) = proximity, closeness
vicit from vinco = he defeated
victor (3) = winner
video (2) = I see
villus (2) = hair
vindex = vengeful
vinco (3) = I defeat
vinum (2) = wine
viola (1) = violet
violentus/a/um = violent
vipera (1) = viper
vir (2) = man
visito (1) = I visit
vita (1) = life
vivo (1) = I live
vix = scarcely
vobis = to you
vocaverunt from voco = they called
voco (1) = I call
volo (1) = I fly
volvo (3) = I roll
vos = you
votum (2) = prayer
vox (3) = voice

Telling Tales in Latin: Afterword

I hope you have enjoyed reading this second book in *Telling Tales in Latin* series! I thought I would include an afterword which might provide insight into the intentions behind *Telling Tales in Latin* and *Distant Lands*, as well as inspiration and ideas for how to use the book in sessions and classes.

The first *Telling Tales in Latin* book was written mostly during 2012, in the course of a year long pilot with 10 and 11 year olds from Pegasus primary school on the Blackbird Leys estate in Oxford. This pilot was generously funded by the grant-giving charity Classics for All.

The second *Telling Tales in Latin* book, *Distant Lands*, was written during 2015, while teaching a group of brilliant 13 and 14 year old students at Cheney School in Oxford, a large state comprehensive school where my charity The Iris Project runs a Community Classics Centre. I was running a classics enrichment course for this group of students, and introducing them to the story of Ovid's exile inspired me to start to write a second book in the series, this time rooted in a journey and a historical framework. I knew that this would inevitably imbue the stories with a more melancholy edge, but I hoped that the readers would be carried along by Ovid's playful tone and magical stories, as well as feeling moved by the sadness of his own biographical tale.

It is of course for the readers to decide if this has worked! I hope very much that both books will be read and enjoyed by many readers of all ages.

Early seeds

The seeds of these two books were planted in my early childhood, as this is where I learned all about the thrill of telling tales. I grew up with an older brother and younger sister. Between the three of us, we soon learned to tell stories of surprise, wonder and terror which kept us entertained for those long school holidays and weekends. Wherever we went, we would always be spinning stories to excite and frighten one another, and the worlds we conjured have never left me.

Like many children, I learned about the myths of the Greeks and Romans long before I learned any Latin; and in fact when I did first learn Latin, it was alongside descriptions of ancient Rome, slaves and masters, with country villas. I remember as a teenager feeling a sense of disappointment that the dark and colourful stories I'd long known did not seem to connect at all to these remote characters who spoke Latin in the text book we used.

I toyed with the idea of creating a fiction-based Latin course for some years, and once, many, many years ago, started one which involved a girl waking up in a fantasy world where everyone spoke Latin, and she had to work out the language to find her way home! Nothing ever came of that half-completed course, but the desire to create a book which would introduce Latin using imagination, games and storytelling remained with me.

I became a doctoral student in 2001 and chose to study Ovid's *Metamorphoses*, exploring how his narrative style is similar to that of the magical realist movement. It therefore seemed entirely natural to me that when I started teaching Latin as part of a pilot in a school in Hackney in 2006, I would use these stories as the springboard. It took another six years for me to actually sit down and turn the ideas, notes and lesson plans into a book!

Why Metamorphoses?

For me, there is no piece of literature I've encountered which has been more imaginative, colourful, mysterious, winding, dark and thoroughly entertaining as Ovid's epic poem. As he declares in his prologue, this book is to tell the history of the world through a fabric of interconnected, magical stories. This in itself carries a suggestive and counter-cultural note; the flamboyant, irreverent, touching and tragic flurry of tales which follow confirms that Ovid's 'grand' poem intends in fact to tease and mock the grandeur of epic poems. It also, though, on a more serious note, tells the stories of the 'smaller' characters and seems to emphasise the everyday passions of people from all walks of life, and celebrate and commiserate with them.

I could think of no better place to choose my stories, no better poem to use to introduce Latin than Ovid's poem and no better narrator than Ovid himself, the eloquent, poetic, imaginative, comic tale-teller who in the end came to a miserable end through his own talent.

Intentions

Telling Tales in Latin and *Distant Lands* are both intended to be storybooks which happens to also include learning Latin, and the size, illustrations, and content have all been designed around that central idea. A consequence of this driving concept has been several decisions I have taken early on which have caused the books to diverge from courses which introduce Latin.

I have minimised the more obviously text-book aspects such practice sentences and exercises as much as possible, and focused instead on the flow of the stories. I have chosen to have Ovid as an exclusive narrator, as I hoped his chatty persona would act as a comforting and entertaining guide through the stories, and also through the grammar.

In his dialogue, I have not avoided using English words which might seem hard for children. I wanted the books to be a discovery of English and Latin words, so it was important to me to remain true to this by including the richness of English vocabulary. I also feel strongly that pupils can step up to the challenges in the book, with support and encouragement. The vocabulary and grammar of the book goes well beyond similar courses, and also well beyond what is needed for the OCR Entry Level Latin examination which it can be used to deliver. This is because the storytelling to my mind requires interesting vocabulary and grammar to give it colour and energy.

Finally, the activities section is written to look and feel like a book rather than a textbook, so it isn't necessarily a list of activities to follow in rounded bullet point suggestions, but a more meandering set of ideas.

These features, I hope, help to create storybooks with all that I would like that to entail; but inevitably, they bring with them challenges. I have written a guide to the first *Telling Tales in Latin* book, which is available to be downloaded for free from the Iris Project website. The aim of this guide is to detail the challenges I found when delivering the book to my class and the things I did to work around these. I have gone through chapter by chapter, providing translations, and explaining in each one the thinking behind the story I chose, and the way it is told.

Final words

Thank you for reading this afterword, which I hope has provided some helpful insight into the thought and intentions behind both *Telling Tales in Latin* books.

All that remains for me now is to re-iterate my thanks and dedication which appear at the opening of this book:

to all my classics centre-dwelling students for their inspirational and entertaining presence; to David Hodgkinson and Nathan Pinkoski for kindly reading a final draft of this book; to Evelien Bracke and David Gimson for reading through multiple proofs, and for providing friendship, support and encouragement with various classical endeavours; to my brother Neil and sister Marianne for a childhood full of tale-telling; to my parents, husband Duncan and daughter Rachel for their love and for putting up with me (and my mum for reading through so many versions of these books!); and finally, to Ovid, for his poetry.

Available in ebook and in a paperback edition

"Really inviting and engaging, with clear explanations and beautiful and
fun illustrations by Soham De . . . Excellent for projects introducing . . . An
inviting, absorbing and embracing learning experience."
The Classics Library

Telling Tales in Latin

Lorna Robinson
Illustrated by Soham De

Ovid's *Metamorphoses*, stories that explore many of the
founding myths of Western literature, have been popular literature
for millennia. In ***Telling Tales in Latin*** they are the perfect
resource for teaching Latin and general literacy skills.

Each chapter introduces one of Ovid's much-loved stories,
encouraging children to begin reading Latin immediately while
exploring the literary and mythic context of the stories. At the end of
each chapter there are suggested activities to help learners to think about
what they have just read. From Daedalus to the story of Orpheus, Lorna
Robinson uses Ovid's stories to teach Latin grammar and vocabulary,
exploring the relationship between Latin and English grammar to
enhance the child's literacy as well as encouraging children's
imaginations by asking them to discuss how Ovid's
hemes are still topical today.

Telling Tales in Latin has been specially designed to
incorporate all the vocabulary and grammar needed for OCR
entry level Latin, Lorna Robinson also provides an ideal introduction
to the inspirational nature of Roman culture, literature,
philosophy and history.

"Combines mythical storytelling with an introduction to Latin,
building grammar and vocabulary." The School Run